I0408688

The Power of Your Voice

Developing an Authentic Communication Style

Table of Contents

Chapter 1. Introduction

Dive into the realm of impactful communication with our special report, "The Power of Your Voice: Developing an Authentic Communication Style". This enlightening journey isn't just about talking; it's about finding the confidence to get your voice heard and expressing your thoughts with authenticity that resonates. Unleash the untapped dynamics of your communication, comfortably share your ideas, and make meaningful connections. This report is a beacon of powerful, personal expression, shining a light on how to turn your words into a tool for change and connection. You won't just learn to speak; you'll learn to speak in a way that matters, connects, and inspires. All because you chose to invest in understanding the power of your voice! Don't miss out on the chance to explore the magic of your voice; with each page turned, you'll be one step closer to discovering your authentic communication style.

Chapter 2. Understanding the Power of Voice

What is voice? We associate it with the sound emanating from our vocal cords, used as a tool to express our thoughts, emotions, ideas, and queries. Although this definition is correct, it barely scratches the surface of what voice truly embodies. Voice is far more than merely sound; it reflects our personality, confidence, feelings, and beliefs. Therefore, harnessing and understanding the power of voice does not merely imply being audible; it's about making an impact, inspiring change, creating connections, and being authentic. To fully grasp the scope of our voice's potential, we must embark upon a multi-layered exploration where we will dissect numerous elements that fulfill the concept of voice.

2.1. The Anatomy of Voice

Let's start with the literal understanding. Our vocal apparatus is an intricate system comprising the lungs, larynx (voice box), and articulators (tongue, lips, and others). The lungs supply an air stream, which is modulated by the larynx and finely tuned by the articulators to produce the unique sounds that constitute our speech. While this system is generally responsible for all human speech sounds, each individual's distinct voice is determined by personal vocal tract dimensions, tension in vocal folds, and articulatory habits.

2.2. More Than Just Sound

Beyond the biological specifics, voice is a reflection of one's self. It serves as an intricate signal carrying a wealth of information about our emotional state, intention, and certain personality traits. The pace, tone, variation, volume, and even accent all contribute to transmitting this information. For instance, a calm and steady voice might be linked with confidence; a loud, fast-paced voice may signal excitement or nervousness. This interplay between voice and perception underscores the strength that voice carries beyond mere words.

2.3. Emotion in Your Voice

Our voices can be strikingly emotional, often revealing feelings we may intentionally attempt to hide. Happiness, sadness, anger, or fear, subtly color our speech, adding a new depth of understanding. Being aware of this allows us to adjust our voice to align with our desired impression, promoting authenticity while conveying our true feelings.

2.4. Voice and Confidence

Confidence can notably heighten the impact of our voice. When we speak with confidence, our voice naturally assumes a firm, clear and persuasive tone. Such voices tend to command attention and are deemed reliable. They inspire, encourage, and convince. Understanding how to embody this confidence can transform your voice into a powerful tool – a beacon of inspiration and influence.

2.5. The Authenticity of Voice

Reliability, trust, and influence through voice are only possible when authenticity is present. People can generally perceive when someone's voice seems forced, fake, or insincere. Authentic voice resonates, significantly aids in ensuring the credibility of your message.

2.6. Speech Patterns and Impact

Speech patterns encompass things like tempo, pitch, volume, and even the language medium used. They play a crucial role in how listeners interpret what you say, aligning your voice with your personality or the appropriate context.

Voice is much like music, relying on tempo (speech speed), volume (loudness), and pitch (high or low frequency of your voice). Variations in these aspects can express various emotions or intentions.

2.7. Transformative Power of Voice

Appreciating your voice allows you to identify and enhance areas that can change its impact. By understanding and tweaking your voice—its sound, delivery style, emotional inflection, tempo, and volume—you can make it more compelling and influential.

2.8. Connecting with Voice

One of the fundamental purposes of communication is connection. Whenever we communicate, we're attempting to connect with an individual or group. A voice that resonates can bridge gaps, break walls, and unify people. Understanding voice in communication underlines the importance of its tone, pace, clarity, and pitch in successfully engaging with and influencing your audience.

2.9. Developing Your Unique Voice

We all have a unique voice and style that form part of our identity. The aim shouldn't be to transform this, but rather to refine it. Building on your distinct voice while integrating elements of impactful communication can result in a voice that is uniquely persuasive and impactful—your authentic voice.

As we end this preliminary understanding of voice, remember that the journey towards a powerful, authentic voice is ongoing. It requires learning, experience, and continuous adaptation. Understanding the power of your voice is not a target destination, but an enlightening voyage. This chapter may be over, but the journey has just begun.

Chapter 3. Exploring Communication Styles

Understanding communication styles is like learning the language of your interaction dynamics. It helps you make sense of how people think and respond, and allows you to adjust your style to communicate more effectively. This exploration will take you through various communication styles and how to harness their potential in your own personal and professional life.

3.1. The Four Communication Styles

There are primarily four communication styles - passive, aggressive, passive-aggressive, and assertive. These are broad categories with a multitude of variations within each. The underlying theme, however, is how responsiveness and assertiveness interrelate.

The Passive Style

The passive style is characterized by high responsiveness but low assertiveness. People with a passive style will often avoid confrontation and struggle to express their feelings or perspective. They usually agree with others to maintain peace, even at the detriment of their own needs or desires.

The Aggressive Style

High in assertiveness and low in responsiveness define an aggressive style. Individuals exhibiting this style are predominantly self-centered, expressing their feelings freely, often overshadowing and disregarding others' needs and feelings.

The Passive–Aggressive Style

A passive-aggressive style is marked by hidden aggression. These individuals may appear passive on the surface, anxious about revealing their feelings, yet display their aggression through subtle actions or innuendo, causing an undercurrent of discomfort and conflict.

The Assertive Style

Assertive communication is the healthiest and most effective style. These communicators balance assertiveness and responsiveness, expressing their feelings, thoughts, and needs clearly and directly, whilst acknowledging and respecting those of others.

Understanding these styles is the first step towards becoming a more effective communicator. However, accuracy of self-assessment can be an issue, given that we might be blinded by our prejudices and assumptions. One useful technique for accurate assessment is soliciting feedback.

3.2. The Power of Feedback

Feedback, when offered constructively, is a powerful tool for personal and professional development. Whether it's a superior at work or a dear friend, they can provide unique insights into your communicative behaviours. High-quality feedback usually includes concrete examples, potential alternatives, and is offered with the intent to support your growth.

Feedback offers a more objective perspective of your communication style. It illuminates blind spots, corroborates self-insights, and provides direction for development.

Yet, these insights are only beneficial when legitimate action is taken towards development.

3.3. Developing Your Communication Style

You don't change ingrained communication styles overnight. It's a process that requires reflection, learning, unlearning, and consistent effort. Here are some steps to get you started:

4 Monitor progress and adjust accordingly: Keep a journal to monitor your progress. Reflect on how your communication style is changing and modify your goals, learning, and practice accordingly.

Fostering an open mind, self-compassion, and steadfast determination can greatly assist in the development of your communication style.

3.4. The Impact of Communication Styles in Relationships

Your communication style impacts every interaction you have. Whether personal or professional, each conversation carries an opportunity to build a deeper connection or create divisions.

In a professional context, an understanding of communication styles can greatly improve leadership effectiveness, teamwork, and efficiency. When styles are mismatched, miscommunication or misunderstanding can occur, leading to tension and reduced productivity.

Intimate relationships are similarly affected. Harmony in a relationship greatly depends on the ability to communicate effectively, understand, and respect each other's individual styles.

In conclusion, discovering and understanding your communication style can be a profound journey of self-awareness and personal growth. It is an investment that could transform your relationships and interactions, empowering you to express your authentic self more effectively.

Chapter 4. The Art of Authenticity

The underpinnings of authenticity and effective communication are grounded in our conscious self-awareness. We are surrounded by fellow humans, varied in color, culture, and conversation, each with their unique voice. The more in tune we are with ourselves, the higher our chances to unearth our own unique, authentic voice. It pivots profoundly, not on the art of imitation, but on the journey of self-discovery. It triggers the vital rhetorical question - what does it mean to be authentic?

4.1. Understanding Authenticity

Authenticity revolves around being genuine, real, and not fabricated. It's about the unpretentious understanding and acceptance of who you are at your core, devoid of societal pretensions. In terms of communication, it refers to conveying your thoughts, feelings, and opinions with integrity and straightforwardness.

Being an authentic communicator isn't equal to saying everything coming to your mind. Instead, it means expressing your thoughts truthfully, constructively, and respectfully. This characteristic is magnetic, pulling people towards you. They hear respect, understanding, and honesty, encouraging them to sincerely engage and reciprocate authenticity.

4.2. Harnessing Authenticity

Discovering your authentic self can be summarised in three dimensions: self-awareness, transparency, and integrity. This triad forms the structure of authentic communication.

1. **Self-Awareness** — It starts with understanding yourself, your motives, values, and emotions. With conscious vigilance over your responses, you begin identifying your communication habits.

2. **Transparency** — After understanding comes sharing. People find authenticity attractive for its vulnerability. Openly articulating your thoughts and feelings builds trust and deeper connections.

3. **Integrity** — The culmination of self-awareness and transparency is the virtue of integrity. It signifies the alignment of your words and actions with your true self, eliminating hypocrisy.

Mapping your everyday interactions around this authenticity framework can provide insightful reflections. Maintaining an authenticity journal can accelerate your progress by offering regular reminders and scope for improvement.

4.3. Building Blocks of Authentic Communication

Four building blocks form the cornerstone of authentically effective communication: listening, empathy, clarity, and respect.

1. **Listening** — Listening actively is synonymous with caring. It indicates a genuine desire to understand the other person. It forms the primal step towards authentic communication.

2. **Empathy** — Understanding isn't enough; feeling the other person's emotions is vital. Empathy amplifies listening by supplementing understanding with feelings, building deeper human connections.

3. **Clarity** — Authenticity demands precise expression. Clarity in your thoughts and expression forms the hallmark of an authentic communicator. It involves being succinct and easily understandable.

4. **Respect** — Respect is the concrete that bonds all the blocks together. Ensuring your communication is respectful—regardless of your own viewpoints—distinguishes each interaction as authentic.

4.4. Authentic Communication in Real World

Two fundamental practices can cultivate authentic communication in real-world settings: congruent communication and constructive criticism.

1. **Congruent Communication** — It involves ensuring your words, body language, and emotions are aligned. Maintaining congruency demands self-awareness and the ability to manage your emotions effciently.

2. **Constructive Criticism** — It signifies your ability to share a different viewpoint or feedback in a blame-free, constructive manner. It demands empathy, clarity, and above all, respect.

4.5. The Barriers to Authentic Communication

Misinterpretations, fear of vulnerability, sociocultural conditioning, and unconscious biases present stumbling blocks to authentic communication. Recognizing and addressing these obstacles is paramount to nurturing your authentic voice.

Incorporate authenticity into your life gradually and persistently. Remember that authenticity emanates from within. Your journey to authentic communication is never-ending, dotted with trials and triumphs. Enjoy the journey, embrace the learning, and understand who you are in the process. This voyage is not just about speaking;

it's about communicating your truth with the world, vibrating with honesty and empathy. Following this path of authenticity can spur meaningful, profound connections, and it all begins with realizing the power of your authentic voice.

Remember, the goal is to be the best version of yourself, not a better version of someone else. As you converse, question whether you're communicating the real you, whether you're doing justice to your unique voice. Sprint forward and embody your authenticity with conviction. It's not what you say, but how you say it that defines the power of your voice. And what could be more powerful than communicating with authenticity?

Chapter 5. Developing Confidence in Communication

Everyone has felt the pressure of a room full of attentive listeners, staring expectantly, waiting for words that can impress, compel, or convince. It's a daunting moment made overwhelming by the gravity of words unsaid, questions unanswered, and stories untold. Developing confidence in communication is an essential trajectory that liberates your voice, setting it aloft, bolting past the hurdles of doubts and apprehensions, connecting, and creating a lasting impact.

5.1. Understanding the Importance of Confidence

Understanding the importance of confidence is crucial in communication. Confidence amplifies the effect of your words, encourages trust, and sparks fascination among the listeners. When you speak with confidence, you convey credibility, competence, and resolve, factors that are fundamental to fostering strong connections with others.

Developing confidence is not a one-night phenomenon, it's a gradual process, an exploration of your inner potential, unseen possibilities, and belief in self. It's about taking small steps on stone pavements of practice, self-improvement amidst stumbles, learning and evolving at every phase.

5.2. Inventorying Your Strengths

Everyone possesses a unique set of strengths. Identifying them is the first crucial step toward cultivating confidence. It's about acknowledging the areas where you shine and leveraging them optimally. It could be your exemplary public speaking skills, your ability to listen and respond insightfully, or your knack for telling captivating stories. Respect your strengths, acknowledge them, and keep honing them diligently.

5.3. Battling the Fear of Dissent

An intense fear of dissent, of misplaced words leading to arguments, or disagreement often holds us back. When these fears take the helm, your voice falters.

Gather courage and power through your fear, and revel in the beauty of differing perspectives. Disagreement and differing opinions are inherently human, leading to growth and inspiring innovation. Welcoming these differences, discerning, and discussing them optimizes collective wisdom and fosters understanding.

5.4. Embracing Constructive Criticism

Criticism, when viewed through the lens of improvement, becomes a powerful tool for progression. While negative feedback can shake the staunchest of resolves, transforming this adversity into an ally leads to tremendous personal growth and shapes an authentic communication style.

Constructive criticism brings the gift of insight, revealing areas that could benefit from additional work. Accept this tool, using it to sculpt your potential into an undeniable strength.

5.5. The Power of Articulation

Articulation is the vessel of your thoughts communicating their essence accurately to listeners. When you articulate, you bring clarity, create understanding, and set the stage for meaningful conversations.

Polishing articulation skills requires a commitment to vocabulary enhancement, understanding sentence structure, and learning the art of narrative flow. Every investment in this skillset reaps rich rewards in the form of increased confidence and potent communication.

5.6. Amplify Your Conversations with Engaging Body Language

Non-verbal cues like postures, gestures, and facial expressions breathe life into conversation, underscoring what words articulate. They're potent storytellers, communicating emotions, assertion, and commitment.

Understand the power residing in these silent communicators, leverage them to reinforce your words and amplify your authenticity. Maintain eye contact, use assertive gestures and stand tall, which signal confidence, thereby not only boosting your confidence but also enhancing credibility in others' eyes.

5.7. The Role of Active Listening

Communication isn't a one-way street; it requires active participation through attentive listening. Active listening allows you to understand and respond aptly, fostering an atmosphere of respect, mutual understanding, and collaboration.

To develop active listening, practice empathy, show interest, and provide feedback. Remember, effective communication goes hand in hand with effective listening.

5.8. Practice Makes Perfect

Repetition leads to perfection. Practice your speeches, presentations, or conversations. Rehearse and seek feedback. Learn from communication veterans, their techniques, and styles. Watch, adhere, and adapt. Dive deep into the world of words, their arrangement, their pauses, their stresses.

Every practice session brings you closer to mastery, and every mastered skill boosts your confidence, paving the way to an authentic communication style.

In the realm of communication, confidence shines brightest. It's a beacon of authority, authenticity, and relatability that navigates your voice past stormy waters of doubts and restrictions, making a lasting impression. It's not just about speaking, but rather about speaking with a purpose. It's about weaving together thoughts and words with the threads of self-belief, spinning a narrative powerful enough to inspire, connect, and leave a lasting impression. Embrace its potential, harness its power, and treasure the impact it can create.

Chapter 6. Emotional Intelligence and Your Voice

When embarking on the quest to improve our communication, one powerful insight stands out: Authentic communication is more than words and grammar; it is a holistic system highlighting emotional intelligence as its cornerstone. Recognizing and managing our own emotions and those of others is paramount to developing a truly authentic and impactful communication style.

6.1. Recognizing Emotion in Yourself

The first stage of developing emotional intelligence is learning to identify our emotions. Before we can use our voice effectively, we must strive to develop an extensive emotional vocabulary. Often, we react to a scenario without acknowledging what we're feeling. Being able to name our emotions instead of simply experiencing them allows us to gain control over them, ultimately leading to smarter decisions.

However, simply acknowledging our feelings is not enough; we also have to appreciate their depth and complexity. Emotions aren't binary, and they're seldom isolated. They ebb and flow, overlapping and influencing each other. We may feel a combination of joy and anticipation, resentment, and relief. Recognizing these subtleties assists in understanding ourselves and our communication approach better.

6.2. Understanding the Origin of Emotions

Our emotions are a result of our thoughts, experiences, and

perceptions. To engage positively with the world, we must figure out what triggers specific emotions within us. Do particular environments make us nervous? Do certain phrases annoy us? Understanding these triggers arms us with the ability to manage our responses better.

Repeated self-reflection eventually leads us to detect patterns in our emotional responses, helping us predict and control them. This self-understanding is empowering. Not only will our communication improve, but our overall well-being will also be bolstered.

6.3. Managing Your Emotions

Mastering emotions is a two-step process. The first is grasping your immediate emotional response – your emotional reflex, and the second is managing your ongoing emotional reaction – your emotional echo. Often, the difference between successful and failed communication lies in the gap between reflex and echo.

Emotional reflexes are automatic: they represent one's immediate gut reaction. The emotional echo, conversely, is a more prolonged response, controlled and moldable. When you feel your heartbeat rise after someone upsets you, that's your emotional reflex. But, if you remain upset for days, that's your emotional echo.

Having control over your emotional echo is vital in authentic communication. It involves responding rather than reacting. To manage your emotional echo, try techniques such as deep breathing and mindfulness. Reflecting on the situation from another person's perspective can also be helpful.

6.4. Empathy: Recognizing Emotion in Others

Having forged an understanding and control over our emotions, the next step is to develop insight into others' feelings. This is where empathy comes into play. Empathy is about opening our minds to others' emotional experiences and fostering harmonious interactions.

To cultivate empathy, engage in active listening. Focus on the speaker and show them you're interested. Ask follow-up questions to clarify points; repeat or paraphrase what the speaker says to ensure you understand; and provide regular, relevant feedback.

Remember, people often communicate more with their body language than their words. Assess their facial expression, tone of voice, and gestures to gauge their emotional state. Over time, this knowledge will grant you the wisdom to respond empathetically, fostering harmonious interactions.

6.5. Emotional Intelligence in Your Voice

Emotional intelligence directly impacts the authenticity and effectiveness of your voice when you communicate. Your understanding, management, and expression of your emotions help shape how others perceive you.

Emotions often carry over into our tone, pacing, and volume, as well as the words we choose. For instance, when we're stressed, our voice might become hurried or unusually high-pitched. When we're confident, our voice tends to be steady and composed. Being aware of these subtle shifts and using them intentionally can greatly enhance the impact of our communication.

Collectively, understanding the realm of emotional intelligence and its connection to our voice empowers us to view the world through a broader lens. It allows us to perceive the underlying emotional currents in our interactions, enabling us to fine-tune our responses and infuse our conversations with genuine understanding and empathy. Ultimately, this leads to a more authentic communication style that not only speaks but resonates.

Chapter 7. Body Language and Non-Verbal Communication

The most profound way we communicate isn't always through our words, but rather through our body language and non-verbal cues. Non-verbal communication plays a significant role in how we express and interpret intent, and it's crucial to cultivate a mastery of these skills to harness the power of your voice fully.

7.1. Understanding Body Language and Non-Verbal Communication

Non-verbal communication is a non-word communication that involves body language, facial expressions, and other physical cues. Let's take a tour through each one, understanding their particularities and determining how stronger body language can reinforce your verbal message and increase the effectiveness of your communication.

One of the first stops along this journey is eye contact. Making and sustaining eye contact can demonstrate your attentiveness and interest in the conversation at hand. It also suggests that you're comfortable in the situation and can help you connect with your conversation partner on a deeper level.

On the other hand, refusing to make eye contact might signal you're not interested in the conversation or you're not confident about the topic. While eye contact is integral in non-verbal communication, it's important to remember not to let it stray into staring, which can make the other person uncomfortable.

7.2. Decoding Facial Expressions

Often, our faces reveal our innermost feelings even before we utter a word. Facial expressions are a prolific source of non-verbal cues. A smile can convey happiness, approval, or goodwill. A frown might suggest dissatisfaction, concern, or confusion. Raising an eyebrow can reflect surprise, skepticism, or intrigue. Understanding these expressions can help you gauge the emotional state of those around you and react appropriately.

7.3. Unfolding the Secrets of Body Posture

Good posture manages to convey a message of attention, respect, and confidence. Standing tall with your shoulders back (without being too stiff or strained) can instantly make you appear more self-assured and engaged. On the contrary, a slouched posture may convey disinterest or low self-esteem.

Physical space can also communicate a multitude of messages. Leaning in indicates interest and engagement, while leaning away could suggest discomfort. Mirroring someone's body language can subtly indicate that you're on the same wavelength, fostering a connection, and fostering trust.

7.4. The Heart of Hand Gestures

Hand gestures can add enthusiasm and clarity to your communications. They can also serve as a barometer for your feelings. Open hands suggest honesty, acceptance, or submission, whereas clenched fists might convey anger, frustration, or determination. Similarly, a thumbs-up signifies approval and positivity, and pointing could symbolize accusation or direct attention to something valuable.

7.5. Power and Impact of Touch

While less common in professional environments, touch still has its place as a potent form of non-verbal communication. A firm, confident handshake can start things off on the right foot in a meeting or interview. Patting someone on the back can show approval or comfort them during tough times. However, it's essential to be mindful that not all people are comfortable with touch, and it's vital to respect personal boundaries.

7.6. Mastering the Art of Non-Verbal Communication

Just as a painter uses various colors and brush strokes to create a masterpiece, so do you have the capacity to use different non-verbal cues to communicate effectively. It is vital to develop self-awareness about your body language and monitor it consciously until it becomes ingrained.

The secret to mastering non-verbal communication isn't about memorizing or mirroring every possible gesture or expression you've learned about. Instead, it's about integrating these elements naturally into your interactions and being mindful not only of your body language but also of how it's interpreted by others.

Remember, the overall aim of understanding body language and non-verbal communication is to support and enhance your verbal messages, thereby creating a complete, authentic, and impactful communication style.

7.7. From Awareness to Effectiveness

A vital step in improving your body language is becoming aware of your current habits. You can do this by observing yourself in different interactions and situations or even video recording yourself in a simulated scenario. You can then analyze your body language and mark areas for improvement.

Take small steps in your journey of altering body language. Start implementing changes one at a time, monitor the response of your peers, reflect on how you felt using this new behaviour, and repeat until it becomes second nature. Remember, it's an iterative process — practice, assess, tweak, and practice again.

In conclusion, Body Language and Non-Verbal Communication are profoundly influential elements of communication. Developing a deeper understanding and command over these aspects will truly unlock your potential for authentic engagement, powerful expression, and meaningful connection - a critical part of your overall journey to discovering the power of your voice.

Chapter 8. Mastering the Magic of Tone and Timbre

Your voice is the instrument through which your ideas and thoughts are auditory realized. It's not only the content of your speech that matters, but also how that speech is delivered. The tone and timbre of your voice can dramatically affect how your message is received by listeners. As we delve into the magic of tone and timbre, we will uncover its capabilities and how to master it for optimized communication.

8.1. The Basics of Tone and Timbre

Tone has to do with the 'flavor' or 'color' of your voice, while timbre refers to the unique sound quality that distinguishes your voice from others. Both play a key role in how we interpret spoken words and perceive the speaker. Hence, knowing how to utilize tone and timbre effectively can dramatically enhance your communication skills.

The tone of your voice can convey emotion, sarcasm, authority, along with a host of other subtleties. Often, the tone you employ can drastically overshadow the actual words you say. In recognizing this power, you become better equipped to convey your messages precisely and authentically.

Equally crucial is the timbre of your voice. Think of it as the unique voice print that separates you from everybody else. Each voice, like a fingerprint, is distinctive in its character, and this is largely due to timbre. It contributes to making the voice pleasant or unpleasant, authoritative or submissive, and calm or excited.

8.2. Defining Your Tone

Before you can master your tone, you first need to understand it. Pay attention to your voice when you are happy, sad, angry, or excited. Every emotion will elicit a specific tone. Once you are aware of these, you can mold and adapt your tone to suit different situations.

Additionally, the audience plays a significant role in tone selection. Speaking with a loved one may require a softer and more nurturing tone, while addressing a team might necessitate a tone of authority and motivation. Remember that your ultimate goal is not always to match your feelings but to serve your listeners and appropriately communicate your ideas and intentions.

8.3. Harnessing the Power of Timbre

Timbre is a bit more complex as it relates to the natural properties of your voice. However, you can still exercise control over it. Practicing vowel sounds and experimenting with different pitches can broaden your range, develop richness, and enhance the unique character of your voice.

Good vocal exercises can strengthen the voice, optimize clarity, and improve breathing. Develop a routine where you vary your vocal timbre - see how high or low you can go, change your pace, and explore your vocal dynamic range. No matter whether your voice is naturally high or deep, there's a unique richness there that can be harnessed for maximum effect in communication.

8.4. Emotional Influence and Tone

Understanding how to effectively use tone to convey emotions is a major part of mastering communication. Even sometimes when your words might say one thing, your tone could be shouting something different altogether. This is because tone has an explicit connection with our emotions.

Each emotion we feel influences the tone of our voice. The tone has a powerful ability to express hidden emotions, feelings, and thoughts without the need for words. When used effectively, it can coax listeners into the right emotional state, making them more receptive to your message.

8.5. The Art of Listening

Effective communication is not just about speaking - listening is equally important. Listen to other speakers and observe how they use tone and timbre in their speech. Notice how their tone changes depending on their mood, audience, or content of their message. You can learn a great deal about effective communication simply through careful observation.

Sitting down with a book and reading out loud can also be a powerful tool for exploring your vocal range. Pay attention to how your voice changes with different characters or scenes, and how altering your tone or timbre can affect the mood of the story.

The magic of tone and timbre extends far beyond voice modulation; it's an instrument of influence, an undercurrent carrying your verbal message to your listeners. Mastering its myriad nuances can transform your voice from a mere vehicle of speech into your very own symphony of powerful, authentic communication. When used with intention and understanding, your voice, with its unique tone and timbre, can become an unrivaled tool in meaningful and impactful expression.

Chapter 9. Effective Listening: The Other Side of Communication

Good communication isn't just about talking; it is also about listening, about embracing silence, about nurturing understanding, and thereby encouraging the interplay between self-expression and empathetic reception.

9.1. The Importance of Effective Listening

At the heart of successful communication is the ability to actively listen. Active listening turns a basic conversation into a probe for deeper meaning, a display of emotional intelligence, and an opportunity for genuine engagement. Active listening is reciprocal respect in verbal form. As you gift your attention to others, you enable not only their voice but also their intention and emotion.

9.2. The Anatomy of Active Listening

Active listening is made up of several components: comprehension, retention, and response. Each of these helps to enrich conversations, transform relationships, and cultivate empathy.

- **Comprehension**: The first step in the active listening process is understanding the speaker's message. Comprehension involves the listeners' analysis and interpretation of the speaker's words, body language, and vocal cues. A successful listener draws on contextual clues to grasp the speaker's meaning fully.

- **Retention**: Retaining information is critical to active listening. Memory serves as a bridge between the listener's comprehension of the spoken information and their subsequent response.

- **Response**: A listener's response validates the speaker's expression. By acknowledging the speaker's message accurately, the listener promotes open and respectful communication.

9.3. Developing Active Listening Skills

Embracing active listening starts with self-awareness. It requires that you remain cognizant of your listening habits and be willing to develop new skills.

1. Ignite Empathy: Endeavor to genuinely understand the speaker's perspective rather than preparing your rebuttal or reaction. Aim to 'walk in their shoes' and appreciate their emotions and experiences.

2. Encourage Open Communication: Ask open-ended questions that prompt detailed responses. Paraphrase and summarize the speaker's points to show your understanding and interest.

3. Stay Focused: During a conversation, many distractions can occur, both internal and external. Shut out these interruptions to remain attentive to the speaker.

4. Show You Are Listening: Use appropriate non-verbal cues such as nodding, maintaining eye contact, and leaning forward slightly to demonstrate your engagement.

5. Remain Neutral: Resist the urge to judge or argue. Maintain a neutral stance and keep your emotions in check to promote a safe and open environment for communication.

9.4. The Benefits of Active Listening

By becoming a successful active listener, you become an effective communicator as well. It can make you a better leader, create stronger relationships, and promote personal growth.

1. Fosters Better Relationships: Active listening fosters understanding and empathy, strengthening personal and professional relationships.

2. Enhances Problem-Solving: Understanding the speaker's viewpoint allows you to better comprehend the problem and enables more effective problem-solving.

3. Facilitates Learning: Applying active listening in educational settings enhances learning. It turns passive lecture halls into active learning environments.

4. Builds Trust and Respect: Active listening is critical in fostering trust and respect. It signals to others that you value their opinion, promoting a positive relational atmosphere.

5. Self-improvement: Active listening offers opportunities for self-improvement. By practicing active listening, you will develop greater emotional intelligence and interpersonal skills.

Effective listening is an art, subtly powerful and graceful. But as with many arts, it requires practice and consistent effort. Strive to listen more, better, and without prejudice. In the end, you're not just enhancing your communication; you're strengthening the bridges between you and the rest of the world.

Chapter 10. The Role of Empathy in Authentic Expression

Effective communication transcends beyond the notion of merely conveying messages. It plunges into the depth of understanding, empathy, and connection. This chapter will unlock the intricate link between empathy and authentic expression, revealing how this connection empowers communication and gives significance to the power of your voice.

To truly comprehend the role of empathy in communication, it is essential first to grasp its fundamental meaning. Empathy refers to the ability to understand and share the feelings of others. It is the capacity to step into someone else's shoes and view the world from their perspective.

10.1. The Interplay of Empathy and Communication

Empathy plays a crucial role in enhancing the emotional aspect of communication. It promotes mutual understanding and encourages a respectful exchange between the sender and the receiver. By developing empathy, one can respond more effectively and authentically to others' emotional cues. An understanding response can engender meaningful connections and generate a constructive conversation.

Where empathy shapes empathetic listening, it also enhances understanding and repartee in communication. Empathetic listening involves paying attention not only to what is being said but also to emotions, body language, and other non-verbal cues. It encourages the person speaking to express themselves openly, fostering an atmosphere of trust and respect.

10.2. Empathy: A Bridge to Authentic Expression

Empathy links directly to authentic expression by influencing the way we express our thoughts and emotions. By understanding others' feelings, we can respond in a way that feels genuine. Being aware of another person's emotional state allows us to navigate the confluence of emotions in a dialogue, maneuvering it towards constructive and positive exchange.

Consider face-to-face communication; empathy lets us perceive and understand the emotions of our interlocutor, enabling us to respond effectively and authentically. The nuances of tone, body language, or facial expressions become clearer, enhancing the sincerity and authenticity of our responses.

10.3. Cultivating Empathy

Cultivating empathy is an essential step in harnessing the power of your authentic voice. It begins with self-awareness, understanding your own feelings, and emotions. Introspection aids in identifying and controlling your emotional responses, making it easier to empathize with others.

Increasing emotional intelligence also enhances empathy. Emotional intelligence refers to the ability to identify, use, understand, and manage emotions in an effective and positive way. Cultivating emotional intelligence encourages empathy, and in turn, more authentic expressions.

Active listening is another tool for nurturing empathy. It involves fully focusing, understanding, responding, and then remembering what is being said. Active listening helps to understand the perspectives of others better, fostering empathy and ultimately leading to more authentic expressions.

10.4. Empathy: A Stepping Stone to Authentic Communication

Empathy is not only a stepping stone to authentic communication; it is its cornerstone. Empathetic communicators create a safe space for dialogue, inviting others to open up and share their thoughts and feelings. In this supportive environment, you express yourself authentically because you mirror the respect and sensitivity your interlocutor has shown.

Empathy, particularly in challenging conversations, demonstrates respects and understanding. It helps to diffuse tension and manages confrontation, essential tools in the quest for authentic communication. It permits the interlocutors to forge a connection, deepening their understanding of each other, and reinforcing the authenticity of their exchange.

Conclusively, empathy plays a pivotal role in driving authentic expression and communication. It allows us to perceive and understand the world from the perspective of others. It encourages self-awareness, emotional intelligence, and active listening, all of which are essential to cultivate authentic expressions. Empathy is, indeed, the touchstone that transforms our communication from mere dialogue into a symphony of understanding, connection, and authenticity. As we delve further into the power of our voice, let us remember this intrinsic link between empathy and authentic expression and use it to guide our communication, making every exchange meaningful and every word count.

Chapter 11. Transforming Your Voice: Steps Towards Authentic Communication

The transformation towards authentic communication begins with embracing, understanding, and expressing your inherent voice. It requires self-awareness, self-acceptance, openness to growth, and a dedication to the process.

11.1. Understanding Your Current Voice

When we talk about voice in the context of communication, we're referring to more than just the sound produced by vocal cords when we talk. Your voice is a combination of your words, tone, body language, and the emotions behind your messages. This intermingling of elements reflects your identity, personality, and experiences.

Begin this transformation journey by identifying your existing communication style. Take note of the language you use – is it formal or casual? Notice your tone – do you sound bitter, caring, or nonchalant? Pay attention to your body language – are you open or closed off? Finally, tune into your emotions when you communicate. Are you usually calm, angry, sad, or happy?

Understanding your current voice is crucial since it enables you to recognize the areas you need to work on and appreciate the strengths you can build on.

11.2. Embracing The 'Why' Behind Your Voice

Understanding your voice also requires awareness of the motivations behind your communication style. Our voices often reflect our past experiences, learnt behaviors, comfort zones, fears, and even unmet needs.

Take some time to reflect on why you communicate the way you do. Deep dive into your past, connect with your emotions, consider your audience, and question your preferred communication methods.

Address any negative motivations that might be undermining your authentic voice, such as fear of rejection or the need to appease others. Embrace your motivations as they are currently, but also be open to shifting these motives if they no longer align with your communication goals.

11.3. The Shift Towards Authenticity

Shifting to an authentic communication style is a journey, not a destination. It requires consistency in recognition, comprehension, and application. You need to take mindful steps every day to ensure that your voice aligns grammatically with whom you are and how you want to be understood.

Consider integrating practices like mindfulness to stay present in your communication, speaking from the heart to convey authenticity, and actively listening to hear and understand others fully. You should also become comfortable with silence. It doesn't signify emptiness; instead, it offers room for reflection and signals respect for the other person's words.

11.4. Cultivating Self-Acceptance

For your voice to be authentic, it also needs to include self-acceptance. Embrace your imperfections and limitations, celebrate your strengths, and honour the unique contribution your voice brings to the world. The idea isn't to become a perfect communicator but to strive towards presenting yourself as you truly are.

11.5. Expressive and Effective Language

Authenticity also means knowing what you want to say and expressing it clearly and effectively. Understanding language and communication techniques can be a powerful tool to enhance your authentic voice. It's about aligning your body language, tone, and words so that they send the same message. This congruence helps ensure that your message isn't confusing or misleading and maintains your listener's trust.

11.6. The Power of Vulnerability

Vulnerability is integral to authentic communication. It involves opening yourself up to others and sharing your true thoughts and feelings. Vulnerability takes courage but it makes your communication more genuine, relatable and powerful.

11.7. Owning Your Stories

Unleashing the power of your voice also involves owning your stories. Everyone has a story to tell, and your experiences form a significant part of who you are. When you share these stories in your own words, your listeners connect with you in an authentic way.

11.8. Receiving Feedback

Constructive feedback is crucial to this transformation process. The way others perceive us can often offer valuable insights. Seek feedback from trusted individuals who can help you understand how effectively your voice aligns with your goals towards authenticity.

11.9. Cultivating Patience

A transformation towards authentic communication is a process that takes time. Cultivate patience with your progress and remain committed to the journey. While the process might occasionally be uncomfortable or challenging, it's all part of your growth.

By understanding your existing voice and the 'why' behind it, making a conscious shift towards authenticity, cultivating self-acceptance, utilising more expressive and effective language, being vulnerable, owning your stories, welcoming helpful feedback, and maintaining patience through the process, you're ready to transform your voice and embrace authentic communication.

www.ingramcontent.com/pod-product-compliance
Lightning Source LLC
Chambersburg PA
CBHW072220290526

45794CB00007B/2819